Practical
Guided Reading

a toolkit for teaching children to read

By Justin Matthew Lee

Teach Organise Evaluate Modify

CONTENTS

ACKNOWLEDGEMENTS

Firstly, thank you to Judy Taylor (AKA Mrs Wheeler). You have taught me how to be a better teacher. You are the one of the biggest reasons why I could write this book. Some of the ideas are from theory and pedagogy, but so much of it is from you, our teaching and the journey we have shared. My amazing friend and mentor always.

Secondly, I would like to thank Joanna Wright. It has been such a privilege to share this journey with you. With my frequent updates and sharing my excitement every step of the way. Your book, ThinkleSticks (available on Amazon), and our discussions have inspired me to sit down and make the time to write this book and begin a project. You have been my inspiration.

I would also like to thank Tony Burford for reading my *original* first chapter and making me realise what a mess it was! You made me appreciate what a complex task writing a book is. I went back to the drawing board after our discussions and, hopefully, wrote a better book.

Thank you to my cats Apollo and Athena for constantly distracting me whilst writing this. This was particularly useful for when I needed pulling away.

Finally, thank you to Justin Williamson. You have listened to my frequent and daily updates on this book and other crazy ideas. Thank you for supporting me in everything I do.

Chapter 1
Reading Put Simply

In this chapter I will attempt to cover some of the theory, practice and pedagogy of teaching reading to justify the strategy and techniques that I share throughout the book. As I am sure you know, it is always important to have at least a basic understanding of what it is we are teaching, and why. I'm afraid the question, *'how do children learn to read?'* is not an easy one to answer. Additionally, whilst there is theory and research into solving this question we don't fully understand why and how children, or humans, are able to read. We can only base our practice, teaching techniques and strategies on what we do know and what works best for most, if not all, the children in our classes.

Reading is an essential skill for everyday life, without it we would struggle to access much of the world around us. This process does not come naturally, and it is a skill that must be learnt. Mechanically, reading is the process whereby we identify the symbols or letters and assign a verbal sound to the words so they can be spoken and understood. Cognitively, reading is understanding these sounds or words and giving print meaning, then having the ability to process the information. Therefore, children need to be taught two things: firstly, that the letters or symbols are a code that needs to be broken; secondly, that once this code is broken all those words have meaning and convey information.

The Simple View of Reading

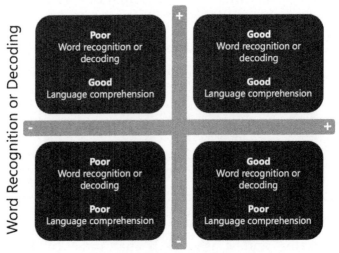

Word Recognition or Decoding

Poor
Word recognition or decoding

Good
Language comprehension

Good
Word recognition or decoding

Good
Language comprehension

Poor
Word recognition or decoding

Poor
Language comprehension

Good
Word recognition or decoding

Poor
Language comprehension

Language Comprehension

The Simple View of Reading (SVoR) spotlight model illustrates this perfectly. This is a very useful tool. Ideally, we want children to be good at word recognition/decoding and good at language comprehension. We can use this spotlight as an assessment tool, which I will go into more detail later. Consider the children in your class and their proficiency at reading; which quadrant would you place them in and why? Guided reading helps to develop and practise the skills for word recognition/decoding and language comprehension. This should be supplemented with a phonics scheme, where the children discretely and actively learn and develop word recognition or decoding.

Word recognition or decoding is about understanding the symbols or letters on the page and assigning them a sound. Once the children have cracked this code, they start to automatically identify whole words. Most adults do this all the time automatically and without realising it. Try this with the following symbols, what does each one mean?

The current teaching strategy that is used for decoding, which is advocated by many, is the systematic teaching of synthetic phonics. Essentially, phonics is about breaking down words into their smallest possible sounds. I will discuss phonics and other cueing strategies later in the book.

Language comprehension is developed in many ways. This is done through book talk and discussion. Through a guided reading session, the children can have this opportunity to discuss and share ideas with peers and the teacher. The teacher can skilfully ask probing questions and engage the children in discussion. This is essentially where guided reading can be used as a powerful tool for teaching reading.

Chapter 2
Overview of Guided Reading

Guided reading is a structured activity led by an adult. It consists of a small group of children having an objective led lesson or session to develop a reading skill focused around a text. Whilst this is happening the rest of the class will be completing other activities to consolidate their skills. It must be objective focused and planned for like any other lesson. Various skills and strategies can be taught during this session discretely. Ideally, the objectives should be taken from the relevant curriculum, for example the National Curriculum or EYFS. The book is then discussed and read, allowing for cueing strategies to be put into practise and time given to develop various responses to the text. Guided reading was advocated by the previous Primary National Strategies and still is by various curricular globally as an instructional method for teaching strategies for reading development and comprehension.

A guided reading session is led by an adult and structured as follows:

Book introduction; reading through the title, discussing the front cover, author/illustrator, reading the blurb, looking at any illustrations on the front cover or in the book, a discussion on the text type, exploration of the features of the text type and any other relevant discussions to give the children confidence to read the book.

Strategy check; a discussion on what to do when a challenging word or sentence is encountered. For example, modelling on the use of phonics or using a glossary to find the meaning of words.

Independent reading; the children should then read at their own pace by themselves. The adult has to listen or *tune in* to each child whilst they are reading. The adult can ask questions during this time to check understanding or momentarily stop the reading for further teaching points.

Returning to the text; a group or peer discussion on the text, which is facilitated by the adult. This is to check the children's understanding of the text.

Re-reading and responding to the text; children complete an activity that demonstrates a thorough understanding or extends their knowledge of the book. For example, writing a character description, answering comprehension questions, drawing a scene from the story or composing a sequel etc.

Each stage is discussed and explained more thoroughly later in the book, but essentially that is it. However, people have adapted this method to suit their own practice and teaching style. When deployed correctly, and modified for your own classroom, it works wonderfully. The children that I teach and the adults that I work with, including myself, thoroughly enjoy their guided reading sessions. I am very aware of the recent stigma that guided reading has gained due to an over complication of the process, the logistics involved and above all the time required. I will provide advice and tips along the way to try to belay or resolve some of these issues. It is important to remember that this is a method for teaching reading. Reading is the cornerstone for every child's education. We have a duty to teach this basic skill to the children or, at the very least, improve upon it during their time with us.

I could continue to list all the problems and challenges that come with guided reading, but I have decided not to do this. This would be a very negative process and tedious for anyone to read. I have just finished reading a book on teaching reading which took this approach, and it read very negatively and as if the teacher did not enjoy teaching children to read. Instead I will go through what I do in my practice and have rolled out successfully. At first it does take time, particularly at the initial stages of development or deployment.

However, in a few weeks you very quickly start to see the benefits. It does require everyone to 'pitch in' with the process. The setup and model I am going to suggest involves a classroom teacher and teaching assistant. I understand that this may be a luxury you do not have, but I can only base this on my own practice and findings.

Initially, and if you have not done so already, you will need to select a guided reading scheme. Ensure that there is a good mix of information or non-fiction texts, narratives and poetry. Whichever one you choose will help to determine which banding, levelling or grading system you use. You will need to decide which year group is going to be at age related expectations (including a greater depth or exceeding level); this is best done based on national expectations, how other schools operate and after discussion and agreement as a staff in your own school. The school I currently work at use a colour banding system and as a team we decided on the following levels or journey.

Colour Band	Attainment Level
Lilac	n/a
Pink A	Nursery for home reader
Pink B	Nursery for guided reading
Red	Reception expected for home (independent)
Yellow	Reception expected for guided reading
Blue	Reception exceeding for home (independent)
Green	Reception exceeding for guided reading
Orange	Year 1 expected for home (independent)
Turquoise	Year 1 expected for guided reading
Purple	Year 1 greater depth for home (independent)
Gold	Year 1 greater depth for guided reading
White	Year 2 age related expectations for end of KS1
Lime	Year 2 greater depth for home (independent)
Copper+	Year 2 greater depth for guided reading

The children will need to be grouped. In order for guided reading to be successful there should be no more than six children in a group, and at least two. With a class of 30 children I aim to create six groups. This can be challenging, and has to take a best fit approach, rather than a perfect fit. The text level or band that the children are reading with you in school should present with some challenge so the child can learn. We have a rule whereby the children take the level or colour below that which they are reading in school during a guided reading session. Here is an example of how the groups might look in my class.

Guided Reading Groups

Guided Reading Colour Band					
Orange	Turquoise	Purple	Gold	White	Lime
Butterflies George Lizzie	**Ladybirds** Tim Rose Alex John Amelia	**Caterpillars** Grace Aiden Mia Emma Liam Sarah	**Ants** Molly Erin Jacob William Amy	**Snails** Aisha Zara Alfie Freddie Toby Michale	**Spiders** Jack Thomas Nancy Martha Willow Louis
Green	Orange	Turquoise	Purple	Gold	White
Home Reading Colour Band					

The teacher will then plan for six groups of guided reading. I will discuss planning in greater detail later. In my classroom the teacher and the teaching assistant will read with a group each; making notes consisting of a sentence or two. This is a little and often approach with focused comments based on objectives taken from the relevant curriculum, assessment frameworks or their aptitude for reading. You could also suggest next steps for the individuals or group. During the following week the teacher and teaching assistant swap groups. The other groups of children will be completing tasks based on developing reading or phonic skills; I will share some ideas for these later. Once the children have finished a reading session with an adult, they complete post reading activities. Which could include re-reading the book and a follow up task. Then the adults move onto the next group in the cycle. I have included an example of a two-week timetable to give a sense of how this might operate in a classroom.

Guided Reading Timetable

Group	Mon	Tue	Wed	Thu
Week One				
Butterflies	Parent Helper	Reading Corner	Guided Reading T	GR Text Follow Up
Ladybirds	Own Book Choice	Phonics Games	Guided Reading TA	GR Text Follow Up
Caterpillars	Reading Corner	Guided Reading T	GR Text Follow Up	GR Text Follow Up
Ants	Phonics Games	Guided Reading TA	GR Text Follow Up	GR Text Follow Up
Snails	Guided Reading T	GR Text Follow Up	GR Text Follow Up	GR Text Follow Up
Spiders	Guided Reading TA	GR Text Follow Up	GR Text Follow Up	Phonics Games

Group	Mon	Tue	Wed	Thu
Week Two				
Butterflies	Parent Helper	Phonics Games	Guided Reading TA	GR Text Follow Up
Ladybirds	Own Book Choice	Reading Corner	Guided Reading T	GR Text Follow Up
Caterpillars	Phonics Games	Guided Reading TA	GR Text Follow Up	GR Text Follow Up
Ants	Reading Corner	Guided Reading T	GR Text Follow Up	GR Text Follow Up
Snails	Guided Reading TA	GR Text Follow Up	GR Text Follow Up	Phonics Games
Spiders	Guided Reading T	GR Text Follow Up	GR Text Follow Up	Reading Corner

Chapter 3
The Reading Journey

The start of a child's reading journey should, ideally, start at home before coming to school. However, it should not be assumed that all children have had access to reading material or been read to. In some cases, a parent reading to their child has been replaced by the television or interactive books on tablets. Children need to be read to and the skills for using a book should be modelled. The children need to know how books work. That they have a front cover, in western culture we read from left to right and that books contain information or a narrative. Many children have developed a good sense of a basic narrative structure, even if they have only been exposed to television. Children should be able to derive pleasure from texts and enjoy listening to stories.

Phonics

The difficulty with the English language is that there are:

- 26 letters in the alphabet,
- 40+ phonemes based on regional dialects or accents,
- over 200 graphemes,
- many words where this code does not work (common exception words),
- and a great number of homophones with the same or different spellings and meanings.

The English language is rich and diverse, and it is an achievement that any of us can speak, read and write it. It is not without question that children have a difficult and challenging task ahead of them.

Initially, the children have to break the code. They need a strategy or technique to help them to make sense of the letters or symbols on the page. The primary method currently used is the use of synthetic phonics. Whether you advocate phonics or not; the research is overwhelming that it is the best possible solution for decoding for 'most' children. The scheme in which you choose to teach phonics systematically is entirely up to you or your school. However, I will refer back to the original Letters and Sounds guidance, as this has been adopted as the de-facto standard by many schools and schemes of work.

The Letters and Sounds guidance sequences the teaching of phonics into six phases. Each one revises and builds on previous learning. The phonics sessions should be fun, engaging and practise the skills of reading and writing. There is a lot of technical vocabulary. On the next page are just some of the words that you might encounter, alongside a definition.

Phonics Glossary

Grapheme – the written representation of a sound or phoneme made up of one or more letters.

Phoneme – the smallest possible unit of sound that makes up a word.

Digraph – two letter grapheme, e.g. *oy*, *aw* or *ay*

Trigraph – three letter grapheme, e.g. *igh*, *ure* or *tch*

Quadgraph – four letter grapheme, e.g. *ough* or *eigh*

Split digraph – where the letter 'e' at the end of the word changes the vowel sound, e.g. *snake*, *flute* or *mike*.

Common exception words – words that are not so easily or impossible to decode using phonics.

Grapheme-Phoneme correspondence (GPC) – the process of identifying that a grapheme makes a phoneme.

Segment – breaking down words into their smallest possible sounds or phonemes.

Blend – to merge the phonemes or sounds together to make a word.

There are many words that are used when teaching or using phonics, however, these are the most common ones that you may or may not have come across. I have listed below a description of each phase to provide a general understanding of the phonics journey the children go through.

Phase One is split into seven aspects. These are environmental sounds, instrumental sounds, body percussion (e.g. clapping and stamping), rhythm and rhyme, alliteration, voice sounds and oral blending and segmenting (e.g. hearing that d-o-g makes 'dog').

Phase Two is when children begin to learn that letters make phonemes or sounds. They are taught the 19 most common phonemes. They learn how to blend and read CVC (consonant-vowel-consonant) and VC words. They also learn some common exception words.

Phase Three introduces children to the remaining phonemes. This includes the introduction of some more digraphs and trigraphs. The children are also taught more common exception words.

Phase Four is where children are not taught any new phonemes. From now on the teaching and learning of phonics is focused on consolidating the skills necessary for decoding and encoding new words. The children begin to use phonics to decode and spell much longer words. They are taught words which have adjacent consonants, including CCVC and CVCC words. The adjacent consonants can sometimes be tricky to hear or sound out, some examples might include *milk*, *belt* or *fact*. They also learn some additional common exception words. Multi-syllabic words are also introduced.

Phase Five takes a lot of time, therefore some people split it into four sections 5a, 5b, 5c and 5d. During this phase the final graphemes and phonemes are taught, including split digraphs; this is where the letter 'e' at the end of the word changes the vowel sound within the word to its letter name. Example words for this include *take*, *these*, *lime*, *stone* or *cube*. Alternative phonemes or pronunciations are taught, for example the letter *'c'* can make a hard or soft sound as in *'cat'* or *'cell'*. The alternative grapheme is also taught; when the same sound or phoneme can have more than one spelling (*ai, ay, a_e, eigh, ey or ei*). More common exception words are taught as well.

Phase Six is where children begin to build up fluency, accuracy and mastery of the phonics skills taught so far. It also teaches spellings patterns, including suffixes, prefixes and contracted words. The children learn less common spellings of words and graphemes.

Once the children have broken the code, they need to have a good understanding of what it is they are reading. Bringing meaning to the text is the next stage of the challenge. Guided Reading allows the children to practise their decoding skills and develop their language comprehension. Children develop language comprehension from a rich and diverse use of spoken English. This has recently become more challenging; especially with the advent of modern technology and the use of tablets or smart phones at the dinner table. The skilful use of questions should be used whilst teaching, alongside high-level discussions with other children and the adults.

The Foundation Stage

The EYFS Statutory Framework very clearly lists what children have to be able to do by the time they leave the foundation stage. The children should have access to a wide range of reading materials, which should include books, poems and other written materials to inspire and *"ignite their interests"*. The children should be able to use their phonics to read decodable words aloud, including reading some common exception words. They should employ their phonic, semantic and syntactic knowledge to understand unfamiliar vocabulary. They should be able to read simple sentences and discuss these with others.

The National Curriculum for Primary Schools in England (Key Stage One and Two)

The National Curriculum breaks down reading into the two strands 'word reading' and 'comprehension' reflecting the Simple View of Reading. The children are expected to progressively use and employ their decoding skills to a point where they are on sight decoding or reading. Eventually, their phonemic knowledge should be applied only to newly encountered words. They should be able to use a range of cueing strategies, including semantic, syntactical and graphophonic knowledge to decode and make meaning of new vocabulary. The children are able to use a range of comprehension skills to infer, predict and make inter-contextual links across a range of genre, authors and texts. They are expected to use and employ these skills in end of Key Stage tests, more commonly referred to as SATs. Guided reading and skilful questioning could also help with scoring and achieving a higher mark in these tests. This is due to the dialogic and discursive nature of the sessions.

Cueing Strategies for Decoding Words or Understanding Vocabulary

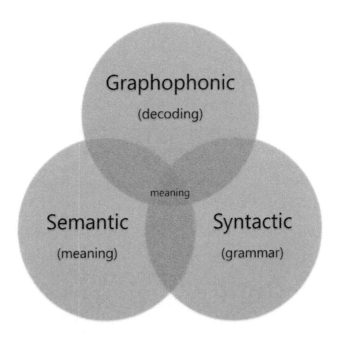

When decoding or trying to understand new vocabulary, children should be taught to look for cues to help them with their reading and turn print to meaning. The model above demonstrates that children employ cueing strategies to help them with this and to bring some meaning. Each one is listed in turn and discussed on how they are used to decode words or to help with understanding the meaning of vocabulary. These strategies are not employed singularly and should be used as a holistic method to attempt to decode a word.

Syntactic awareness is having an understanding of grammar, or the way that the language is organised and structured; or more specifically, the order of the words. Rules are followed in all languages for the order of words when spoken or written. Having a basic understanding of this allows readers to anticipate the sorts of words that might follow after; for example, the *'the blue ball bounced off the wall'* not *'the ball blue wall off the bounced'*. Syntactic knowledge can be developed in many ways, including applying the rules in spoken English. Children can also develop this by re-visiting favourite texts, consolidating their reading of the text and retelling stories. Another way to develop syntactical awareness is through games and activities; for example, reading parts of the story and pausing for the children to complete a sentence that may rhyme - *'Jack and Jill went up the...'*, or fill in a missing word half way through a sentence - *'Jack and Jill … up the hill'*.

Semantic knowledge is finding meaning or an understanding of the text. Being made aware of the type of text and subject matter is essential to understanding the context of what is written. This is important because in the English language we have many words that have several meanings and can even have different pronunciations, for example *lead* and *close*. If readers come across written text that they may not fully understand they may need to re-read it to deepen their understanding. Experienced and wide ranged readers would have a greater knowledge of semantics. To develop semantic knowledge teachers must expose children to different text types and genres. The way they are structured, the use of illustrations, the cover and layout provide clues to what it is we are reading.

The third is graphophonic knowledge and awareness. This includes word recognition, the shape the words or letters make and the use of phonics to decode words. Part of this strategy for word recognition is graphic knowledge, which includes the visual appearance of words. Readers can identify initial letters, word endings, letter strings, word length and word roots to help them recognise words. Children can develop this by looking carefully at words, and matching groups of words or by using onset and rime. A more direct approach with this strategy is through the use of synthetic phonics.

Chapter 4
Planning for Guided Reading

Planning is an important part of any good teaching practice. Before this starts you will need to select a text to focus the session on. The choice should be made whilst considering the children. Choose a text that is going to engage or pique their interest, or a text that could exploit the next steps in their reading journey. After planning for a book, you should centrally store the documents so that all teachers in your school can gain access and retrieve them. That way the teacher will have a plan, any additional resources or activities that have been made, which they can also add to and build at a later date. This way everyone should eventually have a reduced workload. There is an initial push and drive to get the plans done and pool them together. Very quickly you will begin to reap the benefits of this as a collective. The plans can be quickly adapted to suit the children or used straight from the pool. Some guided reading books have plans and activities included with them, either in the back of the book or as an added teacher's guide. These are good for a starting point; however, I would sometimes avoid using them. They are often designed for a much longer guided reading session, not tailored to *your* teaching style or the children you are working with.

I am going to suggest a planning model that will provide for all the necessary components of a guided reading session. This planning format is available to download on my website (www.jmlteach.co.uk). Please feel free to adapt or tailor this method to suit you, your children or your school. Do not be put off by the many boxes and places to write. The idea is that there is a question, a discussion point, a task or activity to go in each box. I have included an example of the planning format.

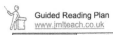

Guided Reading Plan
www.jmlteach.co.uk

Group Name	Caterpillars	Date	05/03/19
Name of Book	Castles	Level/Band	Purple

Word Recognition/Decoding PoS or Objectives (EYFS or NC)

- Read accurately words of two or more syllables that contain the same graphemes as a above.

Language Comprehension PoS or Objectives (EYFS or NC)

- Understand both the books that they can already read accurately and fluently and those that they listen to by:
  - answering and asking questions.

Book Introduction

Questions
Who has ever been to a castle? Which castle? Who lives in castles? Why do you think people built castles?
Discuss the book front cover and the picture of the castle. Read the blurb and discuss what the children want to find out about castles, record questions for later use.

Strategy Check and Independent Reading

Show the children the key words word bank and discuss how to decode each one, and count the number of syllables: castles, moat, drawbridge, portcullis, queen, king, lord, enemy, attack and battlement.
Remind the children to use their phonics and the pictures to help decode any words.

Children to read by themselves. Listen out for points to discuss and share facts whilst reading.

Returning to the Text

Use the questions from the book introduction and see if the children can now answer these.

What else did they find out about castles?
Why are castles built on hills?
What is a dungeon?
What is a garderobe?

Responding to the Text – Post Reading and Follow-up Activity

Children to draw their own castle and add labels.

I have included a space at the top for a group name and the date. Below that is a box for the name of the book, and the colour or level that the children are working on. Next is a space for objectives or programmes of study taken from the EYFS or National Curriculum. This should be your starting point. I will base my examples from the programmes of study taken from the National Curriculum. First, select an objective to focus on for word recognition or decoding, next select another one for developing language comprehension. It is important to choose one or two only, as you will want the reading session to be tightly focused on discrete skills that you are teaching or consolidating.

The next part of the plan is based on the structure for guided reading (I will go into more detail and offer ideas later). You only need to think of a few activities, tasks, questions or discussion points for each area of the plan. I would keep it brief and to the point so that it is an easy plan or guide to follow. To help with activities I have included a task for you to complete based on using Bloom's Revised Taxonomy.

Bloom's Revised Taxonomy

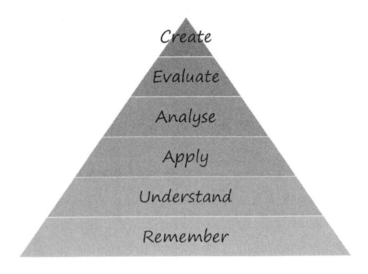

There are many models for learning. However, none are more currently prevalent and advocated than Bloom's Revised Taxonomy. It provides a visual scaffold for children's learning and the processes they have to go through in order to achieve a higher level of thinking or understanding. This model can be applied to guided reading activities and tasks. If you do an internet search you will find many examples of the model, which includes a list of alternative or synonymous verbs that you might find useful.

I will explain the process and give examples and then you can try this using a book of your choice. I am not suggesting that you do this for all the books in your reading scheme; however, this task will be helpful to demonstrate using Bloom's Revised Taxonomy as a tool to help scaffold activities and questions.

Choose a book that you might use when teaching children to develop their reading skills. Create a task for each area, for example, a question, activity or short task for remembering, one for understanding, one for applying... and so on. There is a tool to help you with this that you can download from my website (www.jmlteach.co.uk). Here are some examples of reading tasks for each area of Bloom's Revised Taxonomy to get you started.

Remember
- Where does the story take place?
- Describe the setting.
- Name some of the characters from the story.

- What happens at the end of the story?

Understand
- Using your own words, tell me what the story was about.
- How did the character feel at the start or at the end of the story?
- Draw a picture from the main event in the story.
- Choose an event from the story and discuss why it happened.

Apply
- If you met one of the characters, what questions would you like to ask?
- Choose a character from the story. Discuss an event and what happened to them, including what decisions they made. Would you make the same decisions? What would you have done?
- If one of the characters came to school for lunch, what would you make for them, and why?

- Which character would you like to be friends with, what would you do together, and why?

Analyse
- What happened in the story that couldn't happen in real life? Why do you think this?
- What part of the story did you enjoy the most? What was the funniest part? What was the saddest part? Which part made you laugh, and why?
- Look for and list five contracted words from the story. Why has the author used these?
- Are any of the characters in the story similar to you? Why? How?

Evaluate
- Which character was the villain? Why did they act the way they did?
- A comparison of two, or more, characters in the story.

- Would you recommend this book to anyone? Why and who?
- If you could visit the setting in this story, would you? Why or why not?

Create
- Write a sequel.
- Draw a picture from the story or create a comic strip version.
- Make a wanted poster or a model of one of the characters.
- Choose a character and write a diary from their point of view.

Hopefully, that task helped you to come up with ideas using Bloom's model of learning. The tasks do not have to become more complex as you move up to a higher order level of thinking, they should just engage the learning more. Remember to try and make the activities fun and something that the children will want to do. I go through more examples or activities for each stage of the guided reading session later on.

CROWD Prompts

Another tool that you might want to use for reading, whether this is with a whole class book or during a guided reading session, are C.R.O.W.D. prompts. This an acronym for the following types of questions or discussion points:

Completion: this is where you ask the children to finish the sentence. This is useful for rhyming text, alliteration or repeating patterns in stories.

Recall: ask the children to retell part of the story, recall a fact or part of the events, discuss a character or refer to something they have already read.

Open ended questions: although it is important to use a mix of open and closed questions, open questions allow for discussion and further exploration. The children may have to think more to give an answer.

Wh – questions: questions where you use the words *who, what, when, where* or *why* to explore the text further.

Distancing: this is where you distance the questions from the book whilst making links to real life or to other texts or events.

Returning to the planning sheet, on the back of the plan is a space to record notes on each pupil and general notes for the group. I would suggest taking a little and often approach to this, therefore, it is important to make notes that are clear and useful for later reference. I will go into this in more detail later, when discussing recording and assessment. I have included a brief example of notes that I would keep.

Notes	
Grace	Reading fluently at a good pace.
	Good intonation, needs to develop expression further.
	Able to share facts.
Aiden	Knew about castles, able to share lots of facts.
	Very interested in the book. Good use of expression.
	No overt use of phonics.
Mia	Confident reader, fluent with good use ox expression.
	Able to use the book to share facts.
Emma	Fluent and confident reader, good pace and intonation.
	Some use of phonics to decode.
	Came up with good research question –
	Do only kings and queens live in castles?
Liam	Found some of the text challenging, overt use of phonics.
	Sit next to adult next session.
Sarah	Confident and fluent reader. Good use of expression.
	Able to self correct to check text made sense.
	Didn't share many ideas, even when prompted.
	Discuss book with TA 1:1 later.
General Group Notes	
Group found text suitably challenging. Liam needs monitoring.	

Chapter 5
Book Introduction

The book introduction is an important part of the reading process. You should show the children the book closed, give them a copy and discuss what it might be about before reading. This will help to develop inference, deduction and prediction skills in a more informal manner. You should set the tone that everyone's voice, points of view and opinions are equally shared and valued during the discussion. The adult's job is constantly to act as a facilitator; to ask the questions, engage and encourage the discussions and to share knowledge only when needed. Guided reading should be taught using a *dialogic* model. For this reason, I would suggest operating a 'no hands-up' policy during the session.

The children should begin by discussing the front cover. The title of the book, the author and illustrator, the blurb and any pictures should be discussed before starting to read. This will engage many skills for reading in a more safe and general manner. It is also an opportunity to make links between authors or to discuss different text types and their presentation. All of these tasks may not always be appropriate to the session or the objectives, so choose your questions or activities wisely to capitalise on the learning.

Here is a list of things that you could discuss:

- What is the title of the book?
- Does the title or front cover remind you of anything?
- Discuss any punctuation used on the front cover or blurb. For example, possessive apostrophes, exclamation marks or questions.
- (Pointing to the author or illustrator) who is this person, and why is their name on the front cover?
- Do we know any other books by this author/illustrator?
- Discuss the blurb and any questions there might be.

- What text type is the book? Do the children think this is a narrative, poetry or information text? Why do they think this?
- Would they choose to read this book based on the front cover or blurb? Why or why not?
- Provides a talking point for discussion within the context of the book. For example, if the book is about farm yard animals, ask if anyone has ever been or what animals live there.

After discussing the front cover and the blurb then you could begin discussing what type of text the book is. The *features of the text type* will help with this. The text features will differ according to what type of book you are reading, and it is important to not think that the children will already have this prior knowledge. The features are sometimes so small, underused or skimmed over that the children will need to be reminded of this often. Avoid using the descriptions *fiction* or *non-fiction*; the reason for this is that you can read fictitious information texts or narratives based on real life events etc. I have included a list of some signposts or features for different text types. The list is not exhaustive, and all of these features can be discussed or used as an objective for teaching a whole guided reading session. One example of this might be a session on how to use a glossary and index to help support finding information.

Narrative	Information Text
• Illustrations - drawings	• Pictures, photos or diagrams
• Characters	• Headings
• Plot	• Captions
• Setting	• Contents page
• Dialogue	• Index
• Conflict	• Glossary
• Beginning, middle and end	• Facts
• Chapters	• Running theme

Depending on the text that you are reading and the ability of the children; you might want to do a 'walkthrough' of the book. Whether an information text or a narrative, this is a good way to provide the children with a good overview of the book before reading. If the book is a narrative use the pictures only to try and retell the story in brief. Spend time on a key picture in the text and open up a wider discussion. If the book is an information text then you could discuss the pictures, diagrams and images.

Chapter 6
Strategy Check

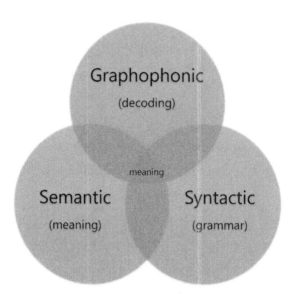

The image above is from a previous chapter (Chapter 3: The Reading Journey). This is an important model to remember when discussing strategies for decoding difficult or newly encountered words and vocabulary. Remind the children to use all three methods; semantic, syntactic and graphophonic to help decode a word or to understand new vocabulary

A word bank would be an ideal tool to model how to decode words through a strategy. Some guided reading scheme books have key words or useful vocabulary listed ready to use. This could be typed up and enlarged to allow for discussing or modelling a decoding strategy to the children. This is a good opportunity to discuss using phonics, breaking down words into syllables or for applying a context to key words. If we take the example of a book about a farmyard, you cannot just assume that every child round the table has visited a farm, is familiar with animals that live on a farm or the day-to-day jobs that happen there.

It is important to allow the children to use the pictures in a book to help them apply a context to their reading. This also helps with decoding the text. In the past I have seen people cover up pictures using sticky notes so that children are forced to only use their phonic skills to decode. In my opinion, this is not good practice! The pictures are there for a reason and often help to tell the story.

Once the children are reading independently you may need to remind them to use a strategy for decoding or understanding new vocabulary. This could involve a discussion of the word and placing it into context with the book, or within another similar context to help the child to understand the meaning. Sometimes you may just need to tell the children what the word is, or what it means. You should not be afraid to do this if needed. This is better than the child potentially feeling failure due to a challenging word.

Chapter 7
Independent Reading

Ideally, the children should be reading independently and at their own pace. They should read aloud whilst tracking with their fingers. This way you can hear the children's reading; their expression of voice and intonation, it also allows you to follow what they are reading. If the children are able to read quietly or *in their head*, they can do this whilst they are reading by themselves. Some adults might think it is more beneficial or efficient to read as a group, where each child takes a turn to read whilst the others follow. However, the children waiting their turn will either follow, not follow or not listen and then the learning is not as effective. There are exceptions to this, for example when reading play scripts or poetry. Whilst the children are reading aloud your job is to listen or tune in to each child, correct any misconceptions and ask questions along the way. This skill will develop with time and practise.

So, what are you looking or listening out for? You are listening for many things whilst the children are reading. Here is a list of examples and how you might encourage or teach the skill:

Use of phonics, decoding or cueing strategies: Are the children using phonics too much? Is the text too challenging for them to decode or access? Do you need to intervene often to tell them the word? Are they overtly using their phonics to decode, or not? Do you need to remind them of a rule when decoding, such as the split digraph?

Intonation and expression of voice: This is where the reader's voice rises and falls whilst reading in response to the punctuation, dialogue or the grammar of the sentence. This is developed through modelling. Initially, you could discretely identify this through reading dialogue; asking the children to put on one of the character's voices, or by modelling when asking questions with the rise and fall of your voice.

Tracking with fingers: This is a useful skill to practise. It helps the children to keep pace and it helps the adult if the children are struggling whilst decoding a word. The children just need reminders to do this and eventually it will become second nature.

Self-checking or correcting: Are the children checking the sentences make sense? Are they self-checking or correcting? If the child has spent a while decoding the sentence, then they should read it back to check they have understood what is being read. If you hear a child say a sentence incorrectly or it does not make sense ask them to read it again, question what the sentence is about or repeat what they have just said back to them and discuss.

Are the children responding to the punctuation?

Whilst the children are reading you might ask questions to check they have an understanding. If they are reading an information text, wait until they have finished reading an important fact and skilfully question them to find out what they have learned in their own words. Encourage them to use the book to help recall the fact and paraphrase, rather than the child re-reading whole sentences. Ask if they want to find out more or if they have any questions. You might also want to discuss any key vocabulary. If they are reading a narrative, discuss the characters and make inferences. Discuss the characters actions and how it might affect others in the story. Discuss the setting and how it might have changed, and why. This is also a good opportunity to predict or to ask if the story reminds them of any others. Children might be afraid to take risks or get things wrong, so remember to reassure them that their predictions do not have to be right; they have to based on what they have already read or found out.

In any text you could discuss the grammatical devices or punctuation. Such as the use of apostrophes, question marks, commas, inverted commas or why the sentence is written in capitals when someone is SHOUTING!

As well as asking questions and discussing the reading it is also important to make notes. Record anything of interest and take a little and often approach to this. I would usually record one or two sentences per child during a guided reading session. This way by the end of six weeks you will have a comprehensive set of notes on all of the children. Some groups may operate at a very similar level and you may choose to record notes for the whole group instead. Try to link your notes back to the National Curriculum or EYFS objectives, the standards from the Teacher Assessment Framework or general comments relating their disposition as a reader. Comments like *"read well today,"* are generally not very helpful or do not tell you much. Just remember to be concise and make your comments meaningful for later use.

If the child is struggling whilst reading do not be afraid to intervene. You can do this by reminding them of various rules when decoding, for example they may have broken down a diagraph into two separate phonemes. You could model segmenting and blending or clap out the syllables to help break down the word. Watch out for children that try to segment and blend a common exception word. Ultimately, if the child cannot read the word, or if you have decided that it is too tricky for them then do not be afraid to just say what the word is.

Chapter 8
Returning to the Text

Towards the end of the session, and after the children have read part, if not all, of the text you should discuss and check that the children have comprehended what they have read. This is similar to a plenary, but for a guided reading session. This is a good time to round up any questions the children have, discuss anything that is important and check that the children have an understanding. During this stage the adult should facilitate and lead the discussion, you should not be tempted to share opinions or fall into the trap of answering your own questions. Remember, like any good plenary; it should link back to the main objectives and teaching points. You might also ask the children to complete a task with a grammar, spelling or punctuation focus.

Here is a list of example questions, discussion points or tasks you might ask the children to complete:

- Asking the children to find as many words as they can with an apostrophe. Then discuss the difference between the apostrophe for possession and contraction.

- You might ask questions about the author's choice of punctuation, for example, *"why did the author use an exclamation mark here?"*.

- Text, lexical, vocabulary or word choices. Discussing the authors choice of words or the meaning of key vocabulary. For example, using a glossary to find the meaning of a word or identifying vocabulary and discussing if the children think that a better word could have been used?

- Discuss what the book reminded them of. Trying to make inter-contextual links with other texts or stories that the children might have encountered. Traditional tales are often a good starting point for this.

- Discuss how the characters are inter-related in the story.

- Pointing out how many scenes or setting changes there are in the story.
- Answering any questions that children might have had prior to reading.
- 'What if...' questions. For example, what if the child was the main character, would they have solved the dilemma in the same way? What if this was a real event, how would it be solved? What if the setting were somewhere else, what would change?

The list above is by no means exhaustive and you will easily think of ideas based on the book. Try not to overthink this stage of the session and stick to the main points. Some tasks are useful for early finishers, such as finding as many words with the '-ed' suffix or writing down all the characters from the book in the order they appeared. I would plan several short tasks that have the maximum impact for the book or the children.

Once this session is complete you might want to make notes on the group as a whole or any comments that individual children have made. Once again, ensure that this is a little and often approach. The notes are for you as the class teacher to refer back to.

Chapter 9
Responding to the Text
& Post Reading Activities

Once the children have read with the teacher or teaching assistant, they will spend the next two sessions completing follow up tasks which are in response to the text. These tasks or activities should relate to the intended learning outcomes and objectives that were originally stated on the plan or further enhance the children's understanding of the text. They should be engaging and have a purpose. For this I will refer you back to the timetable where you will see that once the children have completed the guided reading session led by an adult (labelled as 'Guided Reading T' or 'Guided Reading TA') they should complete the follow up task (labelled as 'GR Text Follow Up').

Guided Reading Timetable

Group	Week One			
	Mon	**Tue**	**Wed**	**Thu**
Butterflies	Parent Helper	Reading Corner	Guided Reading T	GR Text Follow Up
Ladybirds	Own Book Choice	Phonics Games	Guided Reading TA	GR Text Follow Up
Caterpillars	Reading Corner	Guided Reading T	GR Text Follow Up	GR Text Follow Up
Ants	Phonics Games	Guided Reading TA	GR Text Follow Up	GR Text Follow Up
Snails	Guided Reading T	GR Text Follow Up	GR Text Follow Up	Reading Corner
Spiders	Guided Reading TA	GR Text Follow Up	GR Text Follow Up	Phonics Games

Group	Week Two			
	Mon	**Tue**	**Wed**	**Thu**
Butterflies	Parent Helper	Phonics Games	Guided Reading TA	GR Text Follow Up
Ladybirds	Own Book Choice	Reading Corner	Guided Reading T	GR Text Follow Up
Caterpillars	Phonics Games	Guided Reading TA	GR Text Follow Up	GR Text Follow Up
Ants	Reading Corner	Guided Reading T	GR Text Follow Up	GR Text Follow Up
Snails	Guided Reading TA	GR Text Follow Up	GR Text Follow Up	Phonics Games
Spiders	Guided Reading T	GR Text Follow Up	GR Text Follow Up	Reading Corner

I would also like to refer you back to the task that involved using Bloom's Revised Taxonomy in Chapter 4: Planning for Guided Reading. If you have not completed this task then I would encourage you to have a go, as it will help with this process. Below is an image of Bloom's Revised Taxonomy to refer back to.

Hopefully, you now have a good understanding of the structure of a guided reading session and how the week might look. As discussed before, please tailor this process to suit you, your school and most importantly your children the best.

- A story map or a story mountain – the children could create a story map or story mountain of the narrative.

- Comic strip version – the children could combine images and writing to create a comic strip of the book, they could also use this technique to create a sequel.

- Wanted poster or character description – an alternative example of this for older children could be designing a social media page or website.

- Comprehension questions – the children have a list of questions based on the text that they have to answer. A good tip for those schools or year groups that complete tests is to include the page number that will help to find the answer.

- Drawing one or several scenes from the book.

- Design a new front cover.

- Create a fact file from the book – this could be the whole book or a small section, for example if the book is about dinosaurs,

choosing a favourite and writing about it
with a diagram.

- Creating a 3D model to go with the book.
- Writing a short sequel to the story.
- Writing a news article – choose an event or
  character from the book to report on.
- Drawing a diagram and labelling it – this
  could be a character, or something from
  the book.
- Writing a poem in response to the book –
  an acrostic or a kennings poem to describe
  something.
- Creating simple puppets for the story and
  retelling it verbally.
- Using toys or small world objects to retell
  the story to each other.

I would recommend choosing an activity that is
challenging enough to keep the children on task, but
easy enough to allow for independent working. It
should be quick to explain, simple but effective and
allow for the least amount of disruption for the
whole class. Some guided reading schemes provide
example activities for follow up tasks, and

sometimes in the form of PDF files. These are very useful to have and use.

In terms of marking, assessment and feedback this depends on the task or activity. The children are not going to return to the activity once it is finished, therefore, I would just tick, or *light* mark the work. Then I would file it away as evidence for use when assessing or moderating.

Chapter 10
Assessment of Reading

Reading can be assessed in many ways. If guided reading has been implemented successfully then formative assessment will become a holistic part of the process. The assessment will be ongoing and be taken from your notes. Also, the colour band, stage or level that the children are currently reading at should help to indicate where the child is in his or her journey. However, sometimes a more thorough or summative assessment tool is needed or required. This is particularly useful for the children that are operating below age related expectations, those that are perhaps making small steps to close the gaps in their learning or to diagnose any potential barriers to their children's learning.

The simplest tool to help assess the children is the Simple View of Reading. This can be used to help sort groups and to pin point any gaps in the children's learning, including where you should focus the teaching. For example, if you have a small group of children with poor language comprehension; you could group them together and have a greater focus on discussing, questioning and developing comprehension. If you have a group of children that have poor decoding skills, you could group these together and read more easily decodable text to help develop fluency and accuracy. You can either do this to track a groups' progress or to track individual's progress. It is helpful to use the axis of the Simple View of Reading as a scale. I have included a copy of this assessment matrix on my website to download (www.jmlteach.co.uk) I have included an example where I have tracked the previously exampled guided reading groups in this fashion.

Guided Reading Groups

Guided Reading Colour Band					
Orange	Turquoise	Purple	Gold	White	Lime
Butterflies George Lizzie	**Ladybirds** Tim Rose Alex John Amelia	**Caterpillars** Grace Aiden Mia Emma Liam Sarah	**Ants** Molly Erin Jacob William Amy	**Snails** Aisha Zara Alfie Freddie Toby Michale	**Spiders** Jack Thomas Nancy Martha Willow Louis
Green	Orange	Turquoise	Purple	Gold	White
Home Reading Colour Band					

Simple View of Reading Assessment Matrix

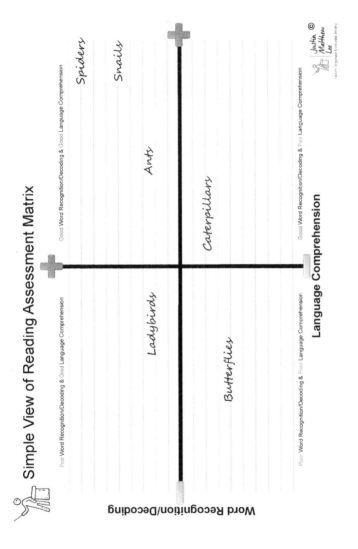

Poor Word Recognition/Decoding & Good Language Comprehension

Good Word Recognition/Decoding & Good Language Comprehension

Good Word Recognition/Decoding & Poor Language Comprehension

Poor Word Recognition/Decoding & Poor Language Comprehension

Spiders

Snails

Ants

Caterpillars

Ladybirds

Butterflies

Language Comprehension

Word Recognition/Decoding

Justin Matthews Lee ©

73

The groups are completely fabricated for the purposes of this book. However, I have hypothetically created real life scenarios and contexts for each group. These are listed below to help further understand the needs of each group based on their placement on the assessment matrix.

Butterflies: This group have poor word recognition and poor language comprehension. The two children within this group are both on the special needs register and have very specific needs.

Ladybirds: This group have poor word recognition and good language comprehension. They are a very talkative and social group of children. However, they did not pass their Year 1 phonics screening check. They are still on Phase 5 and making good progress to close their gaps.

Caterpillars: This group have good word recognition and poor language comprehension. Some of the children in the group have English as an additional language. The children are good at decoding; however, they do not practise their reading at home, some of them talk about using tablets at home and frequently attend after school clubs. This means that they do not read at home as often as would be desired.

Ants: This group have good word recognition and good language comprehension. This group are on track to be at age related expectations for the end of year 2. They are making steady progress. They are supported with their reading at home.

Snails and Spiders: These groups have good word recognition and good language comprehension. They are on track to be at age related expectations and are operating at greater depth. They are supported with their reading at home and read every day. They enjoy reading and read widely.

Sometimes a more thorough assessment of the children's reading abilities might be required to diagnose a gap or barrier to their learning. Initially, this could be done by simply reading 1:1 with the child on a specific text. It might be useful to have a different adult read with them or someone with a wider knowledge and pedagogical understanding of reading. This might help to diagnose the problem. For a more thorough investigation I would suggest using a reading record and a miscue analysis. There are some ready made schemes that you can purchase for this. But you can make your own, for which I have provided a simple template on my website (www.jmlteach.co.uk). It does not have to be the whole book. This will help to identify the fluency, accuracy and comprehension of the text in a structured and systematic way. You might have seen these before.

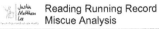
| Book Title: | Little Red Riding Hood | Level: | Green | Word Count: | 250 |

Name: Tim   Date: 25.3.19   Teacher: Mrs. Holland

Page	Text	Error
1	Once upon a time there was a little girl.	1
2	Her name was Little Red Riding Hood.	
3	Her grandma was ill, so she decided to visit her.	2
4	"Don't go into the woods," said her mother.	
5	Little Red Riding Hood knew that the woods were dangerous.	1
6	She also knew that it was a shortcut...	

The child reads the book or text to you whilst you mark what they can read and any errors they might have encountered. Below is a table of codes that you can use and when to count errors.

Running Record Codes

Behaviour	Code	Notes	Error
Accurate reading	There were three bears	Tick the word	no
Omission	‾‾‾ Once upon a time	Place a dash above the word	yes
Insertion	right I'll blow your house down	Write the added word and place a dash above it	yes
Self-correction	SC The witch lived in a cottage	Write SC above the word	no
Teacher/adult helped	T The big bad wolf ate granny	Write a T above the word	yes
Substitution	flew The hot air balloon drifted away	Cross out the word and record the substitution	yes
Sounded out	c-a-t The cat sat on the mat.	Record as a segmented word with dashes	no

There are many other ways to assess reading. One of them is formal testing. Despite testing not being a very popular means to assess a child's ability, particularly for the younger years, it can provide an accurate assessment of what they can achieve by themselves. Some schools purchase testing systems and schemes for this. Years Two and Six have the past National Curriculum tests (SATs) at their disposal.

Chapter 11
Holding Activities

What do the other children do whilst the adults are reading with a group? This is probably the most contentious and challenging part of the guided reading process. Whenever I read or talk to other people about guided reading this is always something they bring up. This is possibly why they are often referred to as *'holding activities'*, which personally conjures up negative image. Nevertheless, this is what they are more commonly called, and I will stick with this name for this grey area of guided reading.

If you choose the activities really carefully and include some that are self-perpetuating then it should be a fairly easy process. The children will need to be trained to be as quiet as possible and focus on these activities. Similar to the follow-up tasks in the *'responding to the text'* phase of guided reading, the tasks will need to be challenging enough to be stimulating, but easy enough for self-regulated learning. In the example timetable below you will notice that there are very few sessions where the children will be working on holding activities.

Guided Reading Timetable

Week One				
Group	Mon	Tue	Wed	Thu
Butterflies	Parent Helper	Reading Corner	Guided Reading T	GR Text Follow Up
Ladybirds	Own Book Choice	Phonics Games	Guided Reading TA	GR Text Follow Up
Caterpillars	Reading Corner	Guided Reading T	GR Text Follow Up	GR Text Follow Up
Ants	Phonics Games	Guided Reading TA	GR Text Follow Up	GR Text Follow Up
Snails	Guided Reading T	GR Text Follow Up	GR Text Follow Up	Reading Corner
Spiders	Guided Reading TA	GR Text Follow Up	GR Text Follow Up	Phonics Games
Week Two				
Group	Mon	Tue	Wed	Thu
Butterflies	Parent Helper	Phonics Games	Guided Reading TA	GR Text Follow Up
Ladybirds	Own Book Choice	Reading Corner	Guided Reading T	GR Text Follow Up
Caterpillars	Phonics Games	Guided Reading TA	GR Text Follow Up	GR Text Follow Up
Ants	Reading Corner	Guided Reading T	GR Text Follow Up	GR Text Follow Up
Snails	Guided Reading TA	GR Text Follow Up	GR Text Follow Up	Phonics Games
Spiders	Guided Reading T	GR Text Follow Up	GR Text Follow Up	Reading Corner

I will list some example activities that I have either seen or used myself. Some of these activities are designed to be self-perpetuating and some are one off tasks. By this I mean that they can be used again and again and do not require marking or little effort from you, other than the initial set up or design.

Independent Reading

This could take many forms. I might ask my greater depth readers to pre-read the book that we are going to discuss in their guided reading session. These children should already be fluent and confident readers, so I am only checking their comprehension of the text. This is not always suitable, for example if we are predicting or discussing grammar.

The children could read in the classroom's reading corner (I will discuss setting one of these up later). Making a free choice of texts from the collection of books. They could read these by themselves. An alternative is to have a small selection of books on the table for the children to read and enjoy. Remember to ensure that the children get to read a good range of texts. This might include poetry, newspapers, information texts, narratives, magazines or even comic books/graphic novels.

Book Boxes and Story Sacks

I am sure that many teachers have come across the idea of a story sack or a book box. A small selection of books is chosen around a theme, this could be a single author, a subject or topic. Toys, games and other appealing things are added to the collection of books to be stored in a bag or a box. I prefer a box, as this can be added to and evolve, you have more space and the books are less prone to damage. When it comes to tidying up, boxes also have the advantage because you can just place everything in much easier.

Book box or story sack themes could include:

- Dinosaurs
- African stories
- Farmyard animals
- Different religions
- Space
- Adventures
- Famous women from history
- Different Families

- Birds
- Nocturnal animals
- Fundamental British Values
- Fairy tales
- Food
- Choose a single author or illustrator
- Poetry
- SMSC
- Around the world, including atlases
- The United Kingdom
- Focus on a single animal, for example bears or cats

Games

A small selection of educational and age appropriate games are always a useful thing to have in class. Many companies produce and sell games with an element of learning. Even snakes and ladders provides good practise for counting. You might want to make your own games, such as a bingo or lotto game to help practise some basic skills. Phonics games are widely available for download. You need to choose the games wisely as they will have to be played quietly. Think how the games can be extended, for example once the children have played a phonics game where they had to find all the words that have a split digraph, they could write some sentences on a whiteboard.

Other Ideas

The children could use this time to practise their handwriting skills. They could even use the time to finish off any work from a previous lesson. Lots of websites and books provide comprehension tasks, with the text to read and questions to answer, that can be completed independently. Whatever you choose for them to do just remember that it should be stimulating enough but not overly challenging.

Chapter 12
Creating a Reading Environment

The Primary National Curriculum for England instructs teachers to develop and foster a love of reading in all the children they teach. As if this ever needed to be a statutory imperative! I will repeat what I have previously stated that reading should be the cornerstone of every child's education. It is essential that your classroom should reflect this.

The easiest way to make a declaration to reading in your classroom is to develop a reading corner. If you do not already have one, then you must invest time and classroom space for this vital area. If you search on the internet or various other social media networks, you will find many attractive and creative reading corners. You need to make sure that it is inviting and celebrates reading. Ensure that there is a good coverage of texts to stimulate all readers. Do not forget that sharing your favourite books and authors is important but remember not everyone has the same tastes.

This area should look like it is owned by or belongs to the children. Make the children responsible for the tidying and maintenance of the area. Check all the books regularly to ensure that they are presentable, and no pages are ripped or tatty. If they are then throw them away; this might sound like a controversial thing to do but the book has clearly been loved and has now served its purpose. Decorate your reading corner with posters of different children's books, or even better, get the children to draw characters from their favourite books and laminate them.

You need books! Lots of different types of books. The children need to see that you love children's books. Children will mostly model behaviours that they see, more so over than what they hear or are told. If they see that you own children's books and enjoy reading and sharing them, they will start to foster this attitude themselves. I always have two different sets of books, the ones that I like to read or teach from and the others are the ones that the children can read and share. You can purchase packs of books cheaply on various website, high street retailers or even second hand book shops. Do not forget to promote every book you read with the children, even if it is not your favourite. I often say to the children this is my favourite book or author to try and promote the book.

Shared reading should form a part of your daily timetable. Routinely, as with many primary school teachers, I will share and read a book to the children at the end of the day. This is a good opportunity to celebrate books, model reading techniques and have a discussion or book talk. It also allows you to share the books that the children may not be able to access due to their reading abilities.

Finally, I would like to thank you for reading my book. I love teaching reading and love to share my passion for children's books with others. I hope that you have found this a useful guide or toolkit. Do not forget to always adapt and tailor other people's ideas and methods for teaching to suit your own. Please visit my Amazon page or website to leave feedback.

Kind regards,
Justin Matthew Lee
www.jmlteach.co.uk

About the Author

Thank you for showing an interest in my book. My name is Justin Matthew Lee. I have worked in education for over 20 years; all my working life. I have worked in many roles and levels in schools, both primary and secondary. I had worked as a teaching assistant, cover supervisor and I have even had a stint as a lunchtime controller. Eventually, I decided to study at Oxford Brookes University. My degree was centred around the Independent Review of the Teaching Early Reading by Sir Jim Rose in 2006, which had a huge impact on the teaching of reading at the time, including the advocation of teaching phonics across the country. Guided reading was promoted by both university studies and the school that I was employed in. However, the guided reading that I was using in school was an adapted version, which was easier to manage.

After several years of teaching at the same school I decided that it was time to grow and move on. Luckily, my previous mentor and Deputy Head had been employed at a school as the Head Teacher and was in need of an English Subject Lead to help make changes across the school and curriculum. Our philosophies for teaching, pedagogy and ideology have always been the same; placing the child firmly at the centre of everything we do. After all, isn't that why we are there as teachers?

One of the teaching techniques that we wanted to introduce was guided reading. The school had not updated some of its practices to align with the current National Curriculum that, at the time, had only been recently introduced. In particular, the teaching of the newly updated English curriculum had not been fully placed into the timetable. We implemented our adapted version of guided reading across the school. We chose a scheme, created a planning format that was linked to the National Curriculum, made it as sustainable as possible and above all else easy to manage. Thankfully, it was a success; the introduction of guided reading helped the children to develop their reading skills to a higher proficiency. Their decoding skills, expression and intonation, inference, prediction and general reading comprehension was developed even further than ever before.

Throughout all of this I was curious to see if it would work. Afterwards, the Head Teacher and I celebrated our successes and we were very satisfied with our knowledge that it worked! We spent the next few years saying that we should *'bottle it'* and sell it on. So here goes - this is my attempt to *'bottle it'*. Another friend of mine, who recently published a book and is currently in the process of launching a new brand, encouraged me to write it down too. I hope you find it useful and helpful.

Justin Matthew Lee BA (Hons) QTS

Other Books by Justin Matthew Lee

Supporting Guided Reading

An accompanying book to Practical Guided Reading aimed at helping support staff teach guided reading. Designed as a reference and a guide to help your support staff deliver a successful guided reading session.
Available from Amazon in Kindle and Paperback
ISBN: 9781080786305

Reading at Home

Reading at Home
a guide to help you support your child's reading

Justin Matthew Lee

A book for parents to help their child read at home.
The book is very easy to follow, colourful and
bright. It provides parents with an overview of
phonics and how to develop language
comprehension and reading skills.
Available from Amazon in Kindle and Paperback
ISBN: 9781080496969

Phonics Flash Cards

The accompanying book to Reading at Home. This book contains all the graphemes and phonemes as flash cards with examples. Alongside the common exception words from Letters and Sounds.
Available from Amazon in Kindle and Paperback

ISBN: 9781081797010

Teach Organise Evaluate Modify

Printed in Great Britain
by Amazon